Contents

Techniques

Intarsia

Intarsia is a technique used to make motif or picture knits, requiring separate balls of yarn to create the different areas of color. It is completely different from stranded knitting. In stranded knitting both of your yarns are carried from edge to edge of your work; with intarsia the yarns go from color block to color block and interlock. On the wrong side of your knitting you will see it does not have the double thickness that stranding has.

Another difference between stranded and intarsia is the amount of colors used per row. In stranded knitting, typically two colors per row are used, but in intarsia there can be just a few colors to many colors per row. Generally intarsia is knit in stockinette stitch, but other stitches can be added too.

The main technique with intarsia is the twist or interlock of one color to the next. Twisting is one term often used for intarsia but a better term is interlock. In this booklet, twisted will refer to something tangled up! If you do not interlock your color changes, you will produce holes in your work.

Knitters seem to love or hate intarsia. In order to love intarsia you need to embrace the fact that

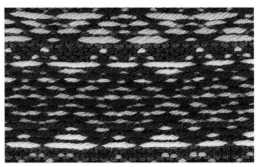

▲ Back of stranded knitting

there could be many yarns to deal with and ends to work in. There are ways to manage all this chaos, and at the end of all your hard work you will produce a beautiful piece of knitting.

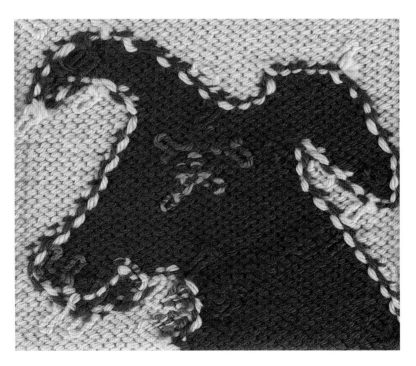

DIVIDING UP THE YARNS

The first consideration when starting an intarsia project is the dividing of your colors. Often knitters will put their yarns onto bobbins. There are various sized and styles of bobbins available. Practice with different ones and see what you like. You can also make a butterfly. A butterfly is made by wrapping the yarns around your fingers, essentially making a small center pull ball. If your yarns get tangled it is easier to pull your small ball apart and rewrap it after the yarns are free.

How to make a butterfly

1. Hold on to to your yarn end with your last three fingers closed over the yarn in the palm of your hand.
2. Wrap your yarn around your thumb and pointer finger making a figure 8. Cut yarn leaving a 8" (20 cm) tail.

3. Carefully slide off your fingers and wrap tail tightly around center of butterfly, sliding the end under last wrap.
4. The butterfly is a center pull mini-skein so pull from the end that was held under your last three fingers.

If you need only a small amount of yarn, two or three yards (meters), do nothing, just let it hang. If you need larger amounts, use the skein or use a center pull ball.

To calculate how much yarn you will need for an area, you can count up the squares on the chart and wrap your yarn around your needle the same amount of times. Remember to give yourself a little extra and for working in your ends. This is just a rough estimate but will get you close. When you make your gauge swatch, you can see how accurate this was and adjust for your project.

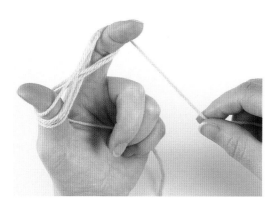 

TWISTING YARNS

There are many ways of controlling your yarns from twisting and tangling. There are bowls and boxes to buy or you can put your yarns in baggies. The trick is to be able to pull your yarns out freely, yet not so much that you have a lot of excess yarn out to tangle. You might find it easiest to do nothing but put all the yarns to your left side. When you have finished working a right side row, turn your needles counter clockwise. You will see with that first knit row you have put a twist onto each yarn. Then when you finish your purl row, turn your needle clockwise and all your yarns will be untwisted.

Do not agonize if your yarns get twisted; continue working as long as you can pull the yarn through. If you get to the point when it's too tangled, then stop and untwist. This is the point where knitters get frustrated, but your yarn does not need to lie perfectly and it is okay for it to be a bit disorderly; you will still produce beautiful knitting. Another frustrating part can be when your knitting is finished and you have to work in all those ends. Put on a good movie or think of it as meditation!

INTERLOCKING

Whether you are on the knit side or purl side the technique is the same. When you come to the point where you want to change colors, hold the color just used to your left and pick up the new color from the row below and place over the yarn just used. Begin knitting or purling depending on which side you are on. Leave the yarn not in use dangling until you are on your next row. Then pick it up and use it again. If you are done with a color, cut it off with a decent length tail to weave in, so there is one less yarn to tangle.

▲ Vertical Interlock Knit

▲ Vertical Interlock Purl

Intarsia designs are not only vertical, but can be organic and move in diagonals. The following pictures show the front and back of the stitches moving left and right. You will see this effect on Rosie Dog pattern and others.

▲ Left Diagonal Knit. Light is dropped to the left; dark is picked up from below and brought over light.

▲ Right Diagonal Knit. Dark is dropped to the left; light is picked up from below and brought over dark.

▲ Left Diagonal Purl. Light is dropped to the left; dark is picked up from below and brought over light.

▲ Right Diagonal Purl. Dark is dropped to the left; light is picked up from below and brought over dark.

You will find that the points where you add and drop colors look messy and you are forming holes. When you work your ends in, all these start and stop points will close and neaten up.

One very important point when interlocking colors is to not be tempted to strand behind a stitch or two because you are trying to cut corners and do not want to add on another new color. The stitches that are stranded will not be interlocked and will fold in and be distorted. Your finished product will not have a consistent appearance.

Sometimes when starting a new color you might miss an interlock. If this happens you can use a tapestry needle and manually interlock it. If you find when your work is done a stitch is slanting in an undesirable way, you can straighten the stitch out with a manual interlock. Use a separate yarn, work in your tail, interlock the stitch, and work in your tail. (Shown at right with orange yarn for clarity.)

If your stitches are distorted, use your knitting needles to manually smooth them out. When locking a vertical line it is not unusual to have a tight stitch then a loose stitch, so again use your needle to manually adjust them. This is often easiest when done from the back by sliding a knitting needle behind the vertical loops.

MIXING INTARSIA WITH STRANDING

First, do not strand from one color block area to another—that will only distort your stitches. Use separate balls for that. But if you want to strand within a motif, this will work. **When interlocking, always make sure that both the stranded colors are being treated as one.** So when interlocking your single yarn it will go over both stranded stitches and the opposite is true when you are interlocking your double strands over the single yarn.

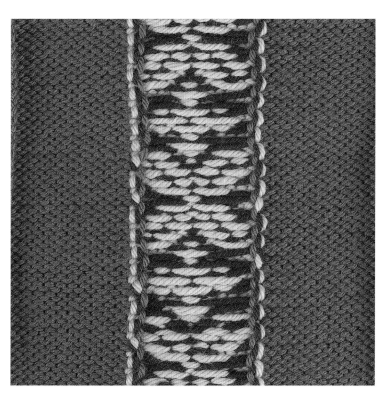

CASTING ON WITH MULTIPLE COLORS

When using a cable cast on, read your chart from left to right. That way when starting your first row, your colors will be oriented in the proper order. The first chart row is both your cast on and your first row. When using other cast ons you may need to cast on reading right to left.

DUPLICATE STITCH

Sometimes a design has one stitch here and there, and to intarsia each individual stitch is impractical. Duplicate stitch embroidery is an easy solution.

WORKING IN ENDS

When learning to knit, one of the first rules learned is to make all your yarn changes at the edges so you won't have a tail to finish off in the middle front of your garment or project. With intarsia you will have ends to work in all over the body of your work, so it is very important to work them in neatly. The best method is to diagonally run your tails through the purl bump. Try to pierce only a small amount (barely a thread) of the bump. Run through three of four stitch bumps, turn, run through three or four more stitch bumps. Running your tails diagonally will help prevent the colors from showing through on the right side, but it also helps keep your knit fabric elastic. One other very important consideration when working in your ends is the amount of tension and direction you will work the tail down. You do not want to pull the tail too hard or you will distort the neighboring stitch, nor too loose. Work the tail down in the direction that closes the hole. A good way to think of this is if you had not changed colors, what direction would this tail have kept working? This is the direction to work your tail in. You will need to determine that with each tail. Sometimes this is quite obvious even from the back and sometimes you have to look from the front and determine which direction closes up and neatens the joined area.

Intarsia Pattern Samples

The following five intarsia projects use a variety of intarsia techniques. The last three: Intarsia Cat, Intarsia Rosie Dog, and Intarsia Heart can be used on the Intarsia Owl Hat project as an alternate to the owl design on page 22.

INTARSIA STRIPE

The most basic of intarsia is a three-color vertical stripe. It is not unusual to have a tight and a looser stitch running up a vertical edge. Manually straighten with a knitting needle pulling the vertical loops on the back side as shown on page 6.

Three colors: A, B, and C.

Intarsia Stripe Chart

▨ = A
▨ = B
■ = C

Cable CO with A, 6 sts, with B, 6 sts, with C, 7 sts, with B, 6 sts, and with A, 6 sts.

Using the intarsia technique, work back and forth in stockinette stitch following chart for color changes.

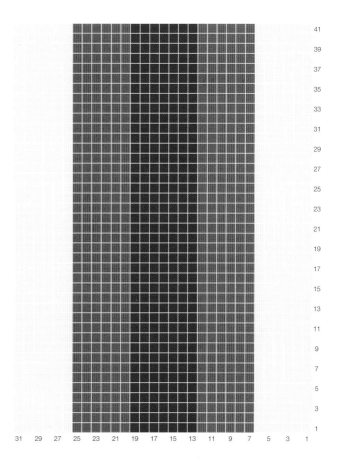

INTARSIA STRANDED MIX

This swatch shows a correct mixing of intarsia with stranding. Notice the stranding is contained within the cream color block. The intarsia interlock happens where the vertical sections meet.

Three colors: A, B, and C.

Intarsia Stranded Mix Chart

■ = A
■ = B
▨ = C

Cable CO 12 sts with A, 13 sts with B, and 12 sts with A.

Using both the intarsia and stranding techniques, work back and forth in stockinette stitch following chart for color changes.

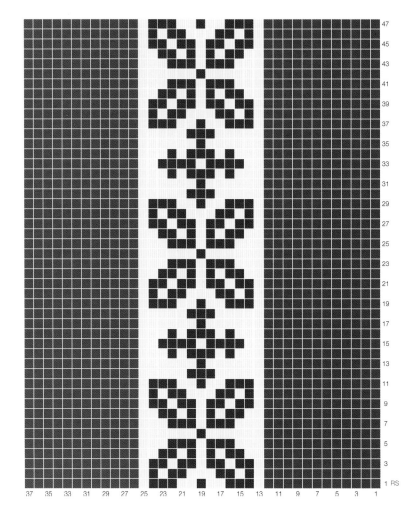

INTARSIA CAT

A cute kitty is the perfect way to practice your intarsia technique. Colors in ears, eyes, nose, and collar are duplicate stitched after the cat's body and background are completed, making this an easy first intarsia. The whiskers are straight stitched on top as the finishing touch. This cat design and chart can be used as a variation to the Owl Hat. If using on the hat, stem stitch the whiskers for more stability.

Six colors: A, B, C, D, E, and F.

Intarsia Cat Chart

= A   ■ = B
■ = C   = D
▨ = E   = F

●——● Straight stitch with C (Note: straight stitch can go between or into middle of stitches.

Cable CO 4 sts with A, 23 sts with B, and 4 sts A.

Using the intarsia technique, work back and forth in stockinette stitch following chart for color changes.

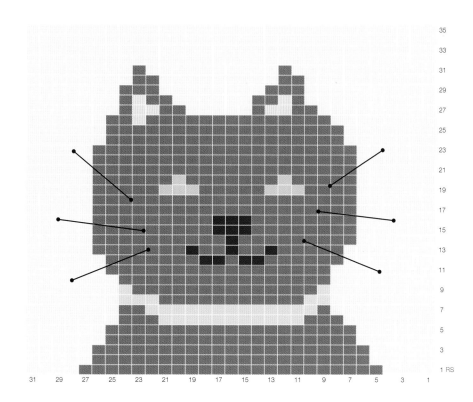

INTARSIA ROSIE DOG

Try out your intarsia skills on this playful pup. To make the intarsia easier, duplicate stitch the eyes, eye brows nose, mouth, and collar when the dog and background are completed. This dog design and chart can be used as a variation to the Owl Hat.

Five colors: A, B, C, D, and E.

Intarsia Rosie Dog Chart

■ = A
▫ = B
■ = C
■ = D
■ = E

Cable CO 19 sts with A and 12 sts with B.

Using the intarsia technique, work back and forth in stockinette stitch following chart for color changes.

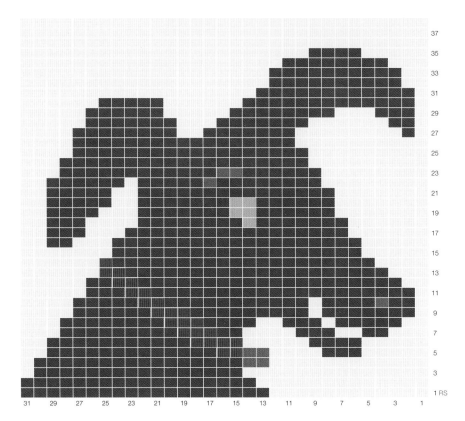

INTARSIA HEART

A three-colored heart design uses the intarsia technique and also incorporates purl stitch texture, in the form of seed stitch. Like the Intarsia Cat and Intarsia Rose Dog, this heart design and chart can be used as a variation to the Owl Hat.

Four colors: A, B, C, and D.

Intarsia Heart Chart

☐ = A
■ = B, K on RS, P on WS
▬ = B, K on WS
▦ = C, K on RS, P on WS
▬ = C, K on WS
▥ = D, K on RS, P on WS
▤ = D, K on WS

With A, Cable CO 31 sts.

Using the intarsia technique work back and forth following chart for color changes and texture stitches.

Intarsia Pillow

This charming pillow is an easy first project. The blocks of color are asymmetrical and alternate from front to back, so by flipping the pillow from front to back or top to bottom, you can change the look on a whim.

MATERIALS

Worsted-weight cotton yarn in five colors

16 " × 16" (41 cm × 41 cm) pillow form

Size 7 (4.5 mm) 24" (61 cm) circular needles

Bobbins (optional)

Tapestry needle

Gauge
16 sts and 22 rows = 4" (10 cm) in Stockinette Stitch on size 7 (4.5 mm) needles

Finished Measurements
16" × 16" (41 cm X 41 cm)

Instructions

With size 7 (4.5 mm) needles and A, CO 66 sts. Work from chart A changing colors as indicated. When chart A is completed do not BO, but begin chart B. BO when chart B is completed.

Block pillow.

Fold the fabric in half along the color change from chart A to chart B. Sew side seams. Insert pillow form. Sew bottom edge.

(continued)

Chart A

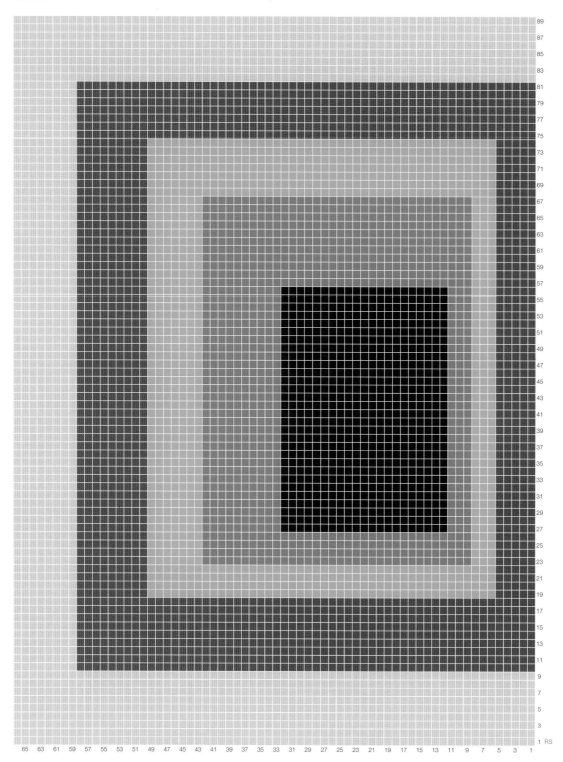

Intarsia Pillow Charts

▨ = A	▨ = D
▨ = B	▨ = E
▨ = C	

Chart B

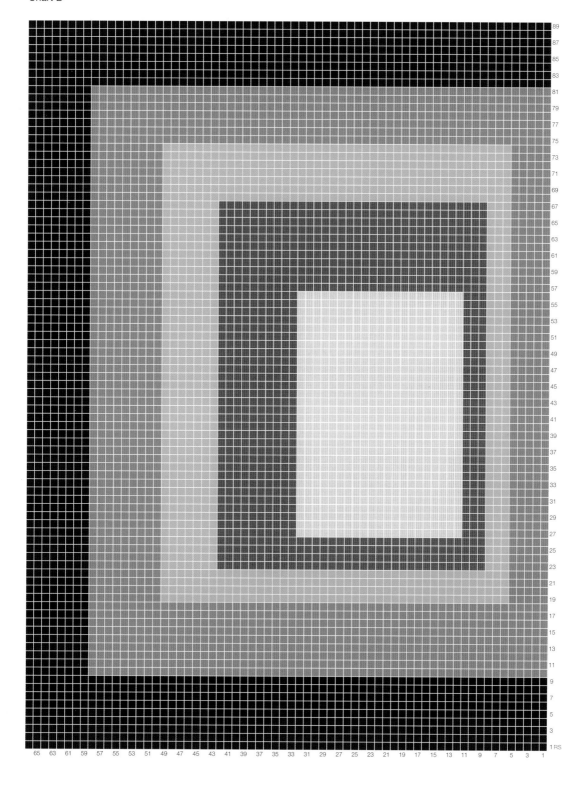

Intarsia Daisy Purse

A sweet daisy flower adorns this pretty purse. To add interest, a coiled I-cord makes for an attractive handle. The green stems and the flower centers can be knit in as you go or could be duplicate stitched on afterwards. Cording is worked into the straps for some extra stability.

MATERIALS

Worsted-weight wool/mohair blend yarn in five colors

Size 6 (4.00 mm) needles straights and double points or size to obtain gauge

Bobbins (optional)

Tapestry needle

Cording to put inside straps

Bodkin

Gauge
22 sts and 32 rows = 4" (10 cm) in Stockinette Stitch on size 6 (4.00 mm) needles

Note: This gauge is on the tight side so the purse will be a bit firmer.

Finished Measurements
6" (15.5 cm) high × 12" (30.5 cm) wide at base, narrowing to 10" (25.5 cm) at top

Note: To construct this purse, knit one side, then pick up stitches from the bottom and work the second side. There are two different types of cast on. The first decision is which cast on you would like to use. If you use a traditional cable cast on, there will be a slight ridge on the bottom edge of the finished purse. This is not a big issue; feel free to use this cast on if you want. However, another choice is to use a provisional cast on. If you use a provisional cast on, you will have live stitches to pick up and you will not have a ridge. Directions for provisional cast on are on page 30. If you use the provisional cast on, when you pick up your live stitches to work the second side of the purse you will be one stitch short, so on that first row of the second side you will need to increase one stitch.

(continued)

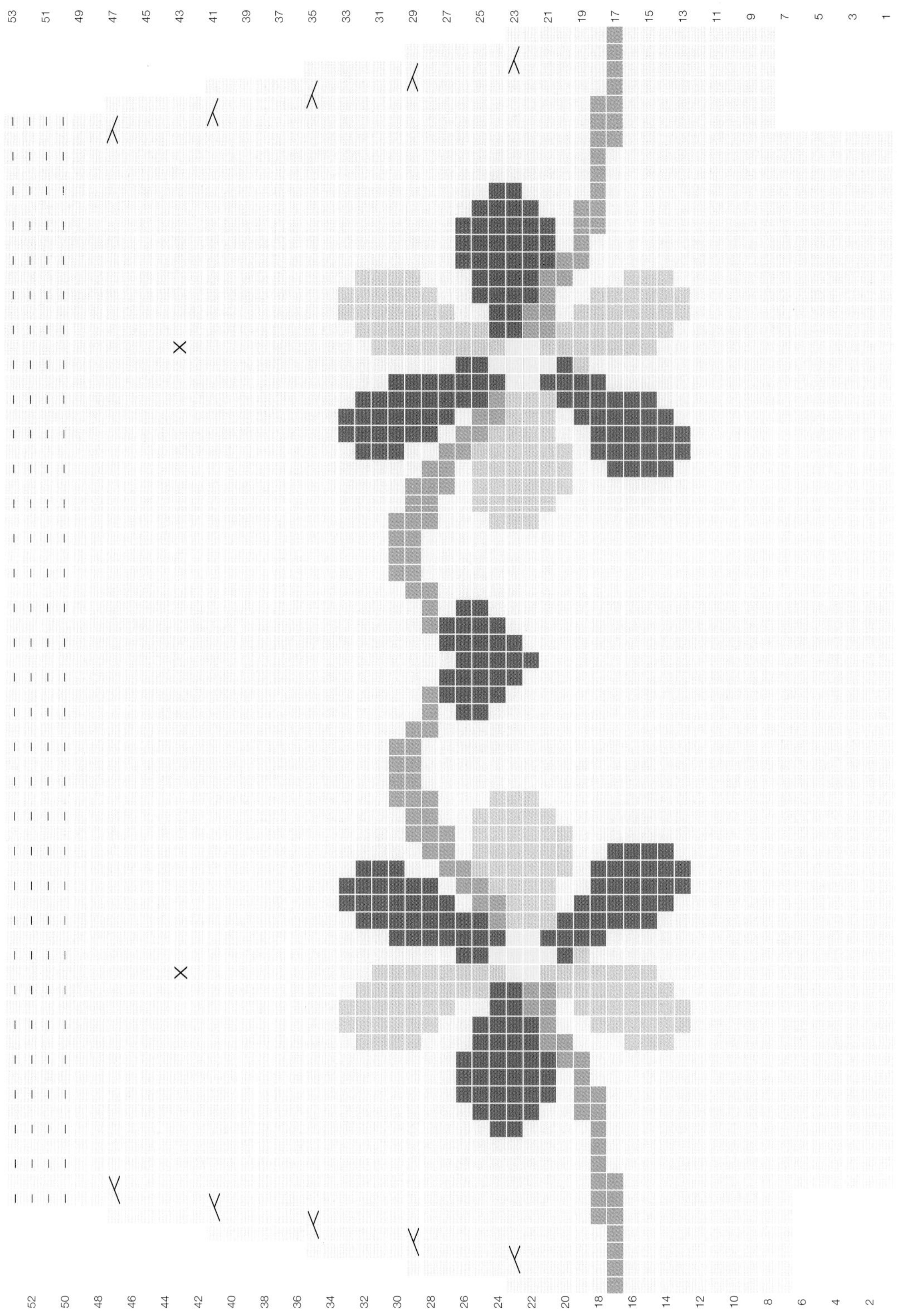

Intarsia Daisy Purse Chart

= A

= B

= C

= D

= E

= k2tog

= ssk

X = attachment point for coiled straps

– = p on RS, k on WS

Instructions

With size 6 (4 mm) needles and A, CO 61 sts using either a traditional or provisional CO.

Follow chart for shaping and color changes.

To make the second side, turn upside down, either PU 61 sts if you used a traditional CO, or if using the provisional CO, release the waste yarn and PU the 60 live sts, remembering to increase one stitch on the following row. Follow chart for second side.

Block. Sew side seams. Sew bottom side seam gusset.

Straps (Make 2)

With size 6 (4 mm) dpn needles and A, CO 5 sts and make I-cord for 32" (81.5 cm). Directions for I-cord on page 141. Leave 12" (31 cm) tails for sewing straps to the body of the purse. With a bodkin, pull 2 or 3 pieces of cording into straps (number of pieces depends on the thickness of your cording). Make sure the cording is worked into the center and does not show on the right side.

Using picture and chart symbol X as a guide, coil and sew down straps to the front and back of purse.

If desired, visit a framing store or artist supply store and buy a piece of matching mat board and cut to fit the bottom of the purse for stability.

Garter Stitch Ribbing

Row 1(RS): *With A, k1, with B, k1, repeat from *.

Row 2: *With B, p1, with A, k1, repeat from *.

Repeat rows 1 and 2.

Intarsia Owl Hat

For a little challenge, try this small project that uses intarsia and stranded knitting techniques combined. At the same time this design is simple and cute! The intarsia samples of Intarsia Cat, Intarsia Rosie Dog, and Intarsia Heart can easily be substituted in the center of this hat, making this four hats in one.

MATERIALS

Sport-weight Alpaca yarn

Size 2 (3.00 mm) needles or size to obtain gauge

Size 3 (3.25 mm) needles (second set for 3-needle BO) or size to obtain gauge

Markers

Bobbins (optional)

Tapestry needle

Gauge

24 sts and 32 rows = 4" (10 cm) in Stockinette Stitch on size 3 (3.25 mm) needles

30 sts and 32 rows = 4" (10 cm) in Stranded knitting on size 3 (3.25 mm) needles

Finished Measurements

Approximately 20" (51 cm) at band, 22" (56 cm) above the band by 7" (18 cm) high

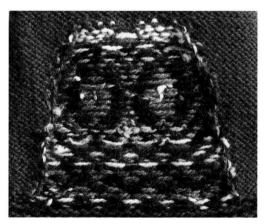

Notes: Hat is knit flat and uses both intarsia and stranded knitting techniques.

All sample design charts (Intarsia Cat, Rosie Dog, and Heart) are 31 sts (instead of 37 like the owl chart). If you want to substitute one of these designs, follow the numbers placed in parentheses. If only one number is given in the direction, then it applies to both the owl chart and any of the sample design charts then it applies to bot.h the owl chart and any of the sample design charts.

A chart is used over the center front 37 (31) sts. Markers are placed on the hat to define these 37 (31) sts.

Pay close attention to the finishing. The hat top has a 3-needle BO in the side-to-side direction. The back center seam is sewn from the ribbing to the top. Next the two top corners are folded and stitched down at the top, at the center back seam.

Tip: Duplicate st the beak and eye centers.

(continued)

Intarsia
Owl Hat Chart

■ = A
■ = C
□ = D
■ = E
▨ = F
■ = G
□ = H
▨ = k2tog
▨ = ssk

Instructions

With size 2 (3.00 mm) needles and B, Cable CO 134 sts.

Work garter stitch rib for 1" (2.5 cm), ending on a WS row.

Looking at the RS of your hat, place markers on your needles counting from right to left: count 49 (52) sts, PM, count 37 (31) sts, PM, end with 48 (51)sts. 134 sts.

Change to size 3 (3.25 mm) needles and A.

Increase Row: Knit 49 (52) sts evenly inc 3 sts, sl m, begin owl chart (using stranding technique and remembering to interlock both stranding yarns from owl to the one yarn of background A, or sample design charts across center 37 (31) sts, sl m, knit 48 (51) sts evenly inc 4 sts (141 sts).

Continue in St st as established following owl chart (or sample design charts) over center 37 (31) sts.

On final row of owl chart 6 sts are decreased. If using sample design chart when chart is completed on next row evenly decrease 6 sts. (135 sts)

When finished with chart continue knitting straight until hat measures 8½" (22 cm). Cut 12" (31 cm) tail.

Set up for 3-needle BO: On back count 34 sts, PM, on front count 67 sts, PM, 34 sts left on the other back half. With RS facing each other place front sts on one needle and two back halves on another.

Using new yarn (not 12" [31 cm] tail) and with the back of the hat facing you, 3-needle BO, top of the hat (page 31). There is one extra stitch on the back needle (side facing you); when you get to the center back opening, BO 2 center back sts together along with one stitch from the front needle, which closes the back seam. See the photo below. Continue binding off to the end. Leave 8" (21 cm) tail.

▲ Place needle into the first 2 sts on front needle and then through first st on back needle. Wrap yarn and pull through all sts.

Using 12" (31 cm) tail sew back seam.

Fold points to the top of center seam, use 8" (21 cm) tails to sew down.

Embellished Butterfly Purse

Everyone needs a small purse, and this one is decorated with an intarsia butterfly, a braided strap, and a long fringe. To simplify the knitting, duplicate stitch the butterfly's outline. The purse is knit in one piece, folded in half and the side seams are sewn. A line of purl stitches at the fold line makes it easy to attach fringe on the bottom.

MATERIALS

Fine/Sport weight wool in four colors

Size 3 (3.25 mm) needles or size to obtain gauge

Size 4 (3.50 mm) needles or size to obtain gauge

Small crochet hook

Gauge
24 sts and 36 rows = 4" (10 cm) in Stockinette Stitch on size 4 (3.25 mm) needles

Finished Measurements
5" (13 cm) wide by 4¼" (11 cm) long (not including fringe)

Purse Body

With A, Cable CO 33 sts.

Work in Stockinette Stitch.

Follow chart, changing needle sizes as indicated and work butterfly motif using the intarsia technique. To make the intarsia knitting easier duplicate stitch color D, the outline around the butterfly.

Block.

Sew up side seams.

Strap

Cut 6 lengths of color A, 1⅞ yds (1.73 m) long. Holding the 6 strands together, knot one end and pin or tape down. Braid two strands in each section the entire length and knot. When finished, machine sew the ends so they will lay flat and cut off knots. A knot will add too much bulk. Whip stitch at least 1" (2.5 cm) of braid to side seams of purse.

Fringe

Cut 30 lengths of color A, 11" (28 cm) long. Using a small crochet hook, insert through center purl bump from back to front. Fold 2 pieces of cut fringe in half, using crochet hook pull through purl bump and make a loop. Place ends through loop and tighten. One fringe made. Continue along one side making the fringe in every other purl bump. Finish other side, 15 fringes total. Trim fringes even.

Embellished Butterfly Purse Chart

Use size 3 needles

= W/A, K on RS, P on WS

= W/A, K on WS

Use size 4 needles

= A

= B

= C

= D

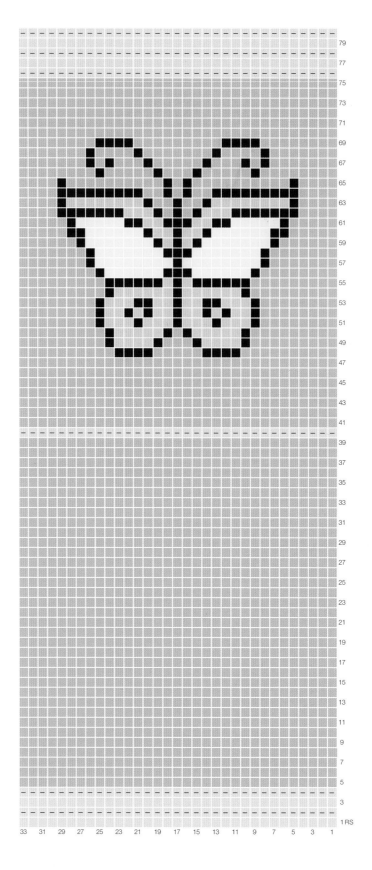

Knitting Techniques

CABLE CAST ON

A wonderful cast on is the Cable cast on. It is decorative and stretchy.

1. Place a slip knot on your left-hand needle. Insert right hand needle into slip knot as if to knit, pull stitch through and place on left-hand needle.

They will unravel without picking the stitches apart and now all the stitches left on the needle look the same. You can use this for flat knitting or for circular knitting. If circular knitting, this area will graft nicely together.

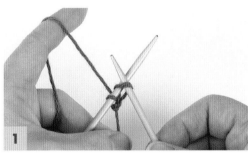

2. Next * insert right-hand needle between stitches, wrap yarn, pull stitch through and place on left-hand needle *, repeat from * to end.

Tip: When using a cable cast on, the first two stitches are a slip knot and knitting into the slip knot, which looks different from the rest of the stitches. Cast on two extra stitches. On your first row of knitting, drop the last two stitches (the slip knot and knitting into the slip knot stitches).

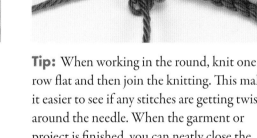

Tip: When working in the round, knit one row flat and then join the knitting. This makes it easier to see if any stitches are getting twisted around the needle. When the garment or project is finished, you can neatly close the opening, matching the slant of the decorative edge. This also works well if you need to put your work on double pointed needles. First cable cast onto a circular needle (any length), knit your first row onto your double pointed needles, evenly spacing your stitches. Join in the next row. This makes it easy to see if any stitches became twisted and will make a neat closure when finishing your project.

PROVISIONAL CAST ON (CROCHETED)

Use this cast on when you want live stitches to work with later. For example, at the bottom of a purse where you will work one side and later go back and work the other side.

1. Using waste yarn, make a slip knot on your crochet hook, leave it on the hook.

2. Hold your knitting needle with the yarn under it and the crochet hook over your needle.

3. Wrap yarn with the hook and pull through.

4. Slide the yarn between the needle and hook, and then around to the back of the needle again.

Continue with steps 3 and 4 until you have enough stitches. With your hook only, chain 2 or 3 more stitches. Cut yarn and pull tail through. Chaining two or three extra stitches at the end will make it easy to see which end to unravel when ready to pick up and knit the other way.

Note: when you unravel and pick up your stitches you will be one stitch short, so increase one stitch.

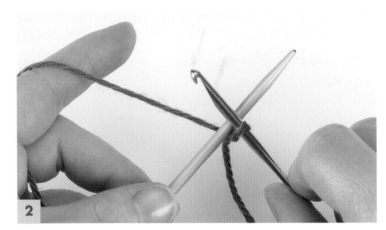

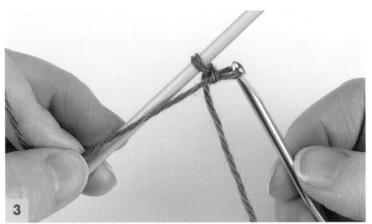

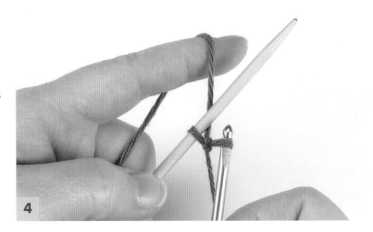

THUMB CAST ON OR INCREASE

▲ Thumb Cast On Right Twist

Right Twist

Start with a slip knot on your right hand needle. To make a twist to the right, twirl yarn around thumb from outside in, insert needle upward through loop and pull off thumb, which makes a twist to the right.

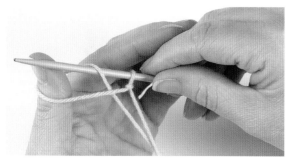

▲ Thumb Cast On Left Twist

Left Twist

Start with a slip knot on your right-hand needle. To make a twist to the left, wrap yarn opposite way, inside out, around thumb, insert needle upward through loop made. Pull off thumb.

THREE-NEEDLE BIND OFF

This bind off is typically used to attach shoulder seams, but in this book it is also used to close pillows, and join the top of a hat.

1. Place stitches to be joined on separate needles.
2. Hold needles right sides together.
3. Using a third needle Insert into first stitches of both needles.
4. Wrap yarn around and pull through both stitches.
5. Slip the stitches off left needles.

Repeat steps 1-5 once more. Two stitches are on your right hand needle. Bind off the first stitch by passing it over the second. Continue in this manner to 3 needle bind off.

I-CORD

Use double pointed needles as you will not turn your work but slide your stitches back to the start/other end of the needle.

1. Cast on 3 sts (or whatever your pattern calls for).
2. Knit 3 stitches.
3. Slip the stitches to the other end of needle, and knit these 3 stitches again.

You will see the working yarn angle across the back. Repeat row 3, and a tube will start forming. Work to your desired length.

TWISTED CORD

To make a twisted cord:

1. Figure out the length you need and cut yarn 3 times that length.
2. Tie a knot on each end.
3. Fasten one end. Have someone hold it for you, or securely tape it down.
4. Slip the other knotted end over a pencil (or a knitting needle) and twist.

Twist until cord folds back upon itself. Bring two ends together and knot. Run your fingers over the cord to smooth it out.

Abbreviations

approx	approximate	p	purl
beg	begin(ning)	p2tog	purl two together
BO	bind off	PM	place marker
CC	contrasting color	psso	past slip stitch over
CO	cast on	PU	pick up
cont	continue	RF	right front
dec	decrease	rem	remaining
dpn	double-pointed needles	RS	right side
inc	increase	sl	slip
k	knit	sl m	slip marker
k2tog	knit two together	ssk	slip, slip, knit two stitches together
k2tog tbl	knit two together through back loops	st(s)	stitch(es)
LF	left front	St st	stockinette stitch
M1	make one	tog	together
M2	make two	WS	wrong side
MC	main color	wyib	with yarn in back
m	meter	wyif	with yarn in front
		yo	yarn over